The
Red Devils

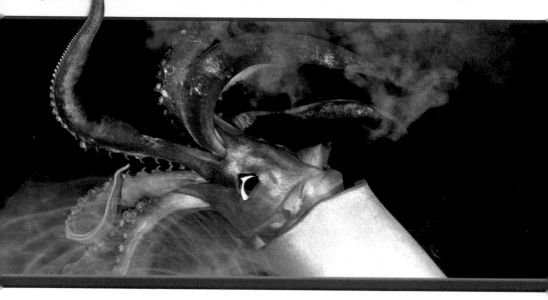

Rob Waring, *Series Editor*

HEINLE
CENGAGE Learning

Australia • Brazil • Japan • Korea • Mexico • Singapore • Spain • United Kingdom • United States

Words to Know

This story is based near the Pacific Ocean and takes place near the Mexican port cities of Santa Rosalia [sɑnta rousɑliɑ] and Guaymas [gwaɪmɑs] on the Gulf of California.

 Giant Squid. Read the paragraph. Then write the correct underlined word next to each definition.

 The Humboldt squid is one of the largest invertebrates in the world and can reach more than 182 centimeters in length and weigh almost 30 kilograms. This dangerous predator is carnivorous and feeds mostly on small fish. It has very long tentacles covered with sharp teeth that it uses to attack. When threatened, these sea creatures squirt streams of dark ink in order to blind their enemies and protect themselves. While their normal prey is limited to small sea creatures, Humboldt squid have been known to eat the bodies of dead fishermen at sea and to attack ocean divers.

1. an animal that lives by killing and eating others: _____

2. a colored liquid usually used in pens: _____

3. meat-eating: _____

4. animals with no backbone: _____

5. animals killed for food by other animals: _____

6. send a stream of liquid out in a thin line: _____

7. long, thin, flexible arm-like body parts found on some ocean creatures: _____

ink

B Deep-Sea Diving. Read the paragraph. Then match each word or phrase with the correct definition.

Neurobiologist Dr. Bob Gilly is going to the Gulf of California in Mexico to study the behavior of the Humboldt squid. His colleague Bob Cranston, an experienced deep-sea diver and intrepid cameraman, is joining him on the trip. Because giant squid live at very great depths, Cranston has developed a special diving device that uses a filter to remove carbon dioxide (CO_2) from his air supply. The special scuba equipment is designed to help him go deeper and stay down longer. The device may also help Cranston avoid the dangerous and sometimes deadly condition of decompression sickness, which results from rising too quickly from the depths of the ocean.

1. neurobiologist _____

2. intrepid _____

3. filter _____

4. scuba _____

5. decompression sickness _____

a. an object that traps unwanted matter as liquids or gases pass through it

b. a sickness caused by a change in air pressure

c. fearless; brave

d. a life scientist who studies the nervous system

e. of or related to using instruments for breathing underwater (Self-contained Underwater Breathing Apparatus)

predator

tentacles

prey

Humboldt squid are sometimes referred to as red devils.

3

When it comes to squid, Dr. Bob Gilly is considered to be an expert. As a neurobiologist at Hopkins Marine Station in Pacific Grove, California, this scientist has studied this fascinating invertebrate for more than 20 years. He's found one squid species, the Humboldt squid, to be truly a giant among the rest. These huge creatures can grow to be up to 182 centimeters* long and live at depths varying from 60 to 180 meters under the ocean's surface. Able to change their color from a deep red to pure white several times in seconds, it is thought that these unusual animals may have developed the ability as part of a complex communication system. These giants of the deep are generally only dangerous when hunting and are often found too far down in the sea to be dangerous to humans. However, they are fierce enough to attack sharks, and when disturbed or threatened, they've been known to be aggressive toward deep-sea divers. It is for these reasons that members of this magnificent species of invertebrates are sometimes referred to as 'red devils.'

In Gilly's most recent study involving the red devils, the scientist **tagged**[1] and tracked the movements of almost 1,000 Humboldt squid off the coast of Mexico, near the city of Santa Rosalia. Two months after the tagging, Gilly discovered that the red devils were appearing across the Gulf of California, near a place called Guaymas. In order to take a closer look at the giant squid and, hopefully, to learn more about them, Gilly is headed over to Guaymas.

---

[1] **tag:** put a tracking device on an animal to follow its movements
* See page 32 for a metric conversion chart.

 CD 1, Track 03

Gilly has big plans for his trip to Guaymas. He's invited a cameraman with him in order to take advantage of the opportunity to film these unusual and **ferocious**[2] giant squid. Bob Cranston is an experienced and intrepid cameraman and diver who has spent more time in very deep water with giant squid than anyone on Earth. Because Gilly does not dive himself, Cranston will serve as the research scientist's eyes underwater so Gilly can get a closer look at the red devils in their own element: the deep waters of the Gulf of California.

In the early afternoon, Gilly meets Cranston at the boat they'll use to bring them out to their diving spot far out in the Gulf. As he arrives, Cranston greets Gilly and begins to give him some details about the new diving equipment he has brought with him. Cranston explains that the new equipment will allow the experienced diver to spend more time under the water in order to do research. In his words, it will allow him to: "[Be] down a little longer, dive a little deeper, get into a little more trouble ..."

The dive won't begin until nightfall, since that's when the giant squid rise from 180 meters below the ocean's surface to just 60 meters below it. The change in depth is attributed to their desire to feed in the more plentiful higher depths of the sea. Luckily, this change of feeding ground also gives Gilly a chance to learn more about them, for although it's deep, a depth of 60 meters is still within a safe range for diving so Cranston can go down and have a look.

---

[2]**ferocious:** vicious; fierce

The wait before the dive gives Cranston and Gilly time to have a look at the beautiful area around the fishing village of Guaymas with its pleasant harbor and fishing boats. "Let's walk up here and talk to these fishermen," suggests Cranston. They decide that it might be a good idea to get the local fishermen's opinion of the giant squid. What they learn is somewhat disturbing news. A local man takes the time to discuss the red devil situation with the two researchers, and it seems that the **jumbo**[3]-size squid are known around here for two things. First, they're known as a source of income, since people can make money fishing for the squid and selling them to markets worldwide as food. The huge invertebrates are also known as something else that's a little more upsetting …

"We lose people. Every other year, somebody dies," reports the local man before adding, "I have a friend that they found floating in the ocean last year." Gilly asks the man if his friend was a squid fisherman and the man confirms that he was before continuing with the story. "It's lucky they found him," he says, "because, you know, [red devils] are carnivorous. They'll eat you, I mean, they will eat you!" Gilly responds in disbelief, "The squid will eat you?" The local man confirms once again, "The squid will eat you. If you fall into the ocean, they'll get you with their tentacles, you'll drown, and then they'll … you know, all the rest of them will just eat you." Could these stories be true? Could the Humboldt be that dangerous? It's enough to worry the bravest of divers and certainly gives Gilly and Cranston something to think about as they prepare for a dive with what may be killer squid.

---

[3]**jumbo:** very large; giant

Fishermen consider squid a source of income, selling them as food around the world.

With the afternoon growing late, it's time for Gilly and Cranston to get down to business. "Okay, time to go diving, sun's going down," Cranston finally says as he begins to prepare to find the giant squid. Gilly and Cranston have created a plan to get as close as possible to the red devils, but it's going to require some major preparations and extremely careful planning.

"Get ready for a night with the squid," Cranston says as he readies the equipment. Cranston knows from his past experience that it can take hours simply to find the squid, possibly requiring numerous dives to 60 meters deep. Traditional scuba equipment is somewhat limited in the amount of air that can be stored and the length of time one is able to stay underwater safely. With such equipment, Cranston could run out of air before having a chance to see a single red devil. So, to avoid running out of air, Cranston will be using a special piece of equipment called a 'rebreather' for this particular dive.

a rebreather

A rebreather is a special device that contains a filter that removes dangerous carbon dioxide from the diver's exhaled breaths while simultaneously adding oxygen. The equipment will allow Cranston to stay under the water longer and to go deeper, but the rebreather also has its disadvantages—and its dangers. The biggest threat is simply staying under too long. "With this rebreather, I can stay underwater up to eleven hours," Cranston explains before adding with a laugh: " It's pretty painful to stay underwater for eleven hours. The maximum I want to stay underwater is about four."

Cranston then discusses where the greatest problem can arise while diving so deep in the ocean. "The real danger is that you don't watch your **gauges**.[4] You get excited about doing something and your oxygen level goes down, down, down," he reports. "And then all of a sudden you pass out because there's no warning of having too little oxygen. Your vision just goes … and then you get black." This scenario is potentially very dangerous, and any diver in such a situation could be very badly injured or even die.

---

[4]**gauge:** a measurement device

The two men head out to where the fishermen have been the luckiest in finding the jumbo squid. Before they start the dive, however, they must wait until **dusk**[5] when the squid rise from inaccessible depths of over 180 meters to a barely accessible 60 meters under the sea. In order to better observe the invertebrates and capture accurate information about these mysterious creatures, Gilly and Cranston are going to attempt an interesting experiment: filming the squid using red light.

Filming jumbo squid is nothing new, but Gilly and Cranston have come up with the unique idea of filming the animals using a different type of light. As Cranston explains, this red light may be especially useful since it can't be seen well underwater. "Red is **camouflage**[6] underwater," he says. "So we're trying to add some red, but still have something we can film with." Cranston then explains that he's using regular camera lights, but has added enough red color to potentially trick the squid into not paying attention to him. Like many deep-**dwelling**[7] creatures, Humboldt squid aren't very sensitive to red light since red is the first color to disappear in the ocean. By using the red light, Cranston will have enough light to film the creatures, but hopefully the light won't disturb the animals as much as a traditional white or yellow light.

---

[5]**dusk:** nightfall; sunset
[6]**camouflage:** a way of hiding something by making it look like its surroundings
[7]**dwell:** live

As Cranston begins to put on his equipment for the dive, it becomes obvious that the lights are not the only things that will be red tonight. Cranston will also be using a red rebreather and wearing a red dive suit in the hopes that he'll be less invasive to the squid's environment. Hopefully, this will allow him to witness more of their natural behavior up close. In fact, with all of his red equipment, one could say that Cranston may fit right in with the squid himself. "I'm going to be a red devil down there," Cranston laughs as he examines his equipment. Gilly joins in the joke saying, "You might never come back. You're going to join them!" The two men seem very relaxed as they do their final checks.

Night has now fallen and the time has come for Cranston to dive into the ocean. It's also time for the joking to stop as things must now get serious. Both men are well aware of the dangers of the dive. Cranston talks a bit about how he feels about his forthcoming encounter with the potentially ferocious red devils as he finalizes his preparations. "I'm not worried about the squid hurting me," he says. "I'm worried about the squid putting up a situation like pulling [my] mask off or pulling a rebreather **hose**[8] off, or something like that. That would be a really bad situation." The red lights may make Cranston less visible to the squid, but there is still a possibility that the creatures may get too close for comfort or become aggressive.

---

[8]**hose:** a flexible tube

Cranston stands at the edge of the boat, inserts the hose from his rebreather into his mouth and checks his gear. He then steps lightly off the side of the boat as Gilly looks on. Cranston pauses for a moment in the black water to turn on his lights and do one more equipment check before he begins his long dive. He then disappears, leaving only a hint of fading red light as he sinks into the darkness.

Diving this deep into the ocean is a dangerous commitment for Cranston. He'll have to spend more than an hour coming up if something goes wrong. If he doesn't take enough time when surfacing, he'll risk getting decompression sickness. In addition, the rebreather weighs over 35 kilograms and makes him less able to move around easily than with traditional scuba diving gear. If there's trouble, Cranston's not going to be able to respond as quickly.

Once Cranston reaches his destination depth, an **eerie**[9] blackness surrounds him, broken only by the faint red lights. The only sound that Cranston hears is that of his rebreather as he waits patiently for the squid to appear. The diver slowly scans the darkness with his red lights and, after a short time, the first squid swim into view. They seem to take no notice of the red light. Then a squid approaches Cranston. Cranston can see it, but can it see him? Apparently it can, but this squid seems more curious than aggressive, using one of its huge eyes to cautiously examine the strange being in its environment. Then, suddenly, a bolder squid comes flying out of the darkness and attacks the camera. Cranston is caught completely off guard.

---

[9] **eerie:** strange; weird

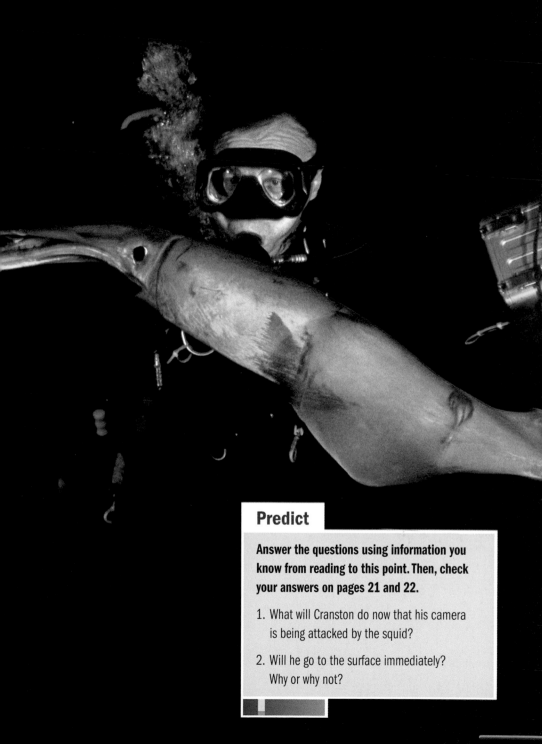

Predict

Answer the questions using information you know from reading to this point. Then, check your answers on pages 21 and 22.

1. What will Cranston do now that his camera is being attacked by the squid?

2. Will he go to the surface immediately? Why or why not?

Suddenly, Cranston is surrounded and attacked by giant squid.

As one squid wraps its dangerous tentacles around the camera, other squid suddenly begin moving towards the diver. The odd-looking animals with their huge eyes and long tentacles seem to be coming towards Cranston and his equipment from all directions—and at top speeds. Humboldt squid can swim between five and thirty-two kilometers per hour, which is extremely fast when one considers that the average human swimmer moves at a pace of only two or three kilometers per hour.

One of the strange-looking creatures attacks Cranston's lights with its tentacles. It grabs tightly onto the bar holding the light and tries to rip it from the diver's hand. Eventually, the animals turn their attention to Cranston himself and his worst nightmare is about to come true. One squid rushes toward him and tries to pull off his mask with its tentacles. Cranston pulls back and there is a fierce struggle. The squid has a firm grip on the only thing that's keeping the man alive so far down in the deep: one slip of the mask and Cranston could be in serious trouble.

Then, as quickly as it all began, the attack is over. The squid swim quickly away, leaving only a squirt of their ink behind, as if to remind Cranston of the encounter. Squid squirt their ink as a way of keeping away possible predators, so they may have been just as scared of Cranston as he was of them. In any case, Cranston is okay, and at last he's able to return to the surface, thankful that he made it out of the uncomfortable situation in one piece.

As he raises himself out of the water and begins climbing back into the boat, Gilly greets Cranston with a cheerful "Congratulations, Bob!" and shakes his hand. When Cranston looks at him in surprise and asks, "About what?" Gilly can only laugh and say, "Coming back!" To this Cranston replies with a smile, "Coming back is good."

Once he gets into the boat, Cranston is characteristically relaxed, almost as if nothing had happened. He tells Gilly his story, but he doesn't seem to imply that it was really scary for him down there. "Well, actually," he tells Gilly jokingly, "I had a squid come and, you know, touch me. They'd **grab a hold of**[10] the camera, and I'd grab a hold of them and kind of shake their hand a little bit." Following this he jokes a bit more with Gilly. "And they'd put out their little tentacles and …," with this he grabs the surprised research scientist by the arm. Gilly reacts with a jump and a small shout before laughing at the joke. The two may find the situation funny now, but it wasn't likely so funny 60 meters below the surface.

---

[10]**grab a hold of (something):** *(expression)* take into one's hand

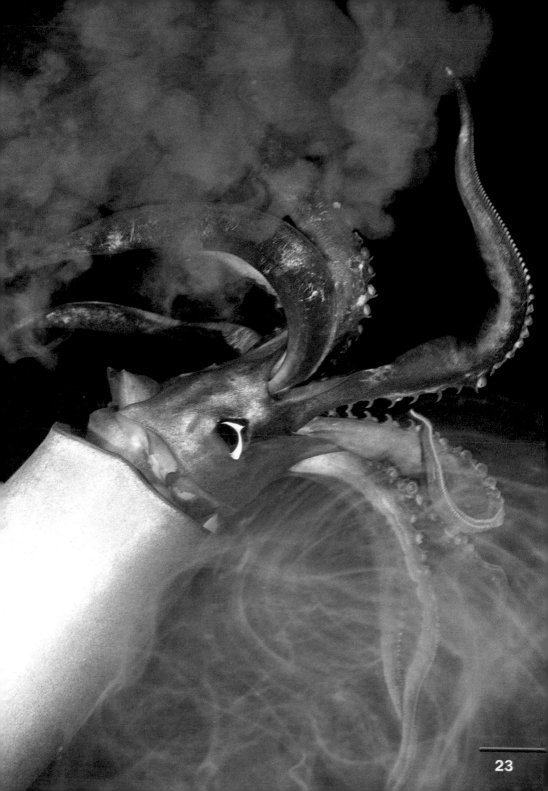

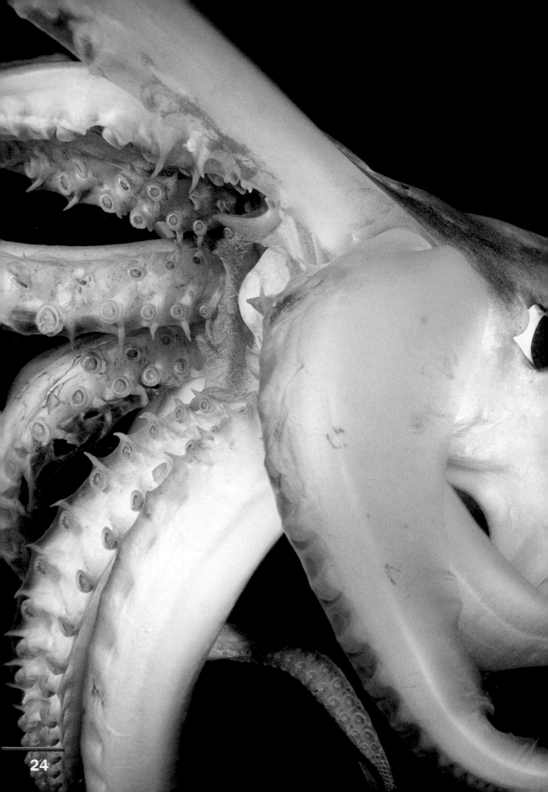

Finally, after all the action is over, Cranston gets to show off his film of the experience to Gilly in the safety of the boat. On a small screen that Cranston has brought on board the ship, Gilly finally is able to see how dramatic the encounter really was. "This was when we had the squid grab a hold of the lights and pull the filters," explains Cranston, pointing at the little screen. "There he comes, right out of nowhere."

As he retells the evening's underwater events, Cranston shares his theory as to how the red devils hunt their prey: "They're coming in at full speed ahead, grab the prey, and full speed reverse. And leave the ink." Seeing this behavior 'live' through the view of the camera is very valuable to a scientist like Gilly. It provides him with an opportunity to actually see how the squid behave in their natural environment.

After watching the fascinating film of the red devils, the two men decide that the red light was definitely a great success. Even though the squid could obviously see it, it's clear that they approached much closer to the camera and equipment than they would have if it were white light. Cranston has managed to capture some **superb**[11] images and Gilly has learned much more about the captivating behavior of these amazing creatures.

Seeing the attack behavior of the Humboldt squid has helped Dr. Bob Gilly to further understand something important about the creatures that he's studied for so many years. "It makes you suspect that they have incredible intelligence," he clarifies, "to see this exploration-type behavior. And I certainly believe they have a lot of intelligence." After seeing the encounter with Bob Cranston and his equipment, it's easy to believe that these animals may indeed be quite intelligent. The discoveries found on research trips like Gilly's not only add to scientists' knowledge bases about these mysterious animals, they may also add to the world's fascination with the ocean's red devils.

---

[11] **superb:** excellent

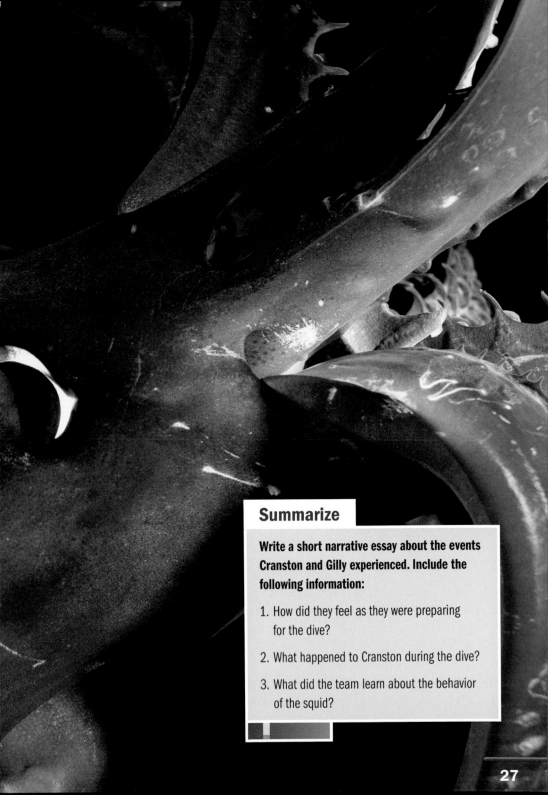

Summarize

Write a short narrative essay about the events Cranston and Gilly experienced. Include the following information:

1. How did they feel as they were preparing for the dive?

2. What happened to Cranston during the dive?

3. What did the team learn about the behavior of the squid?

After You Read

1. What's one reason Humboldt squid are called 'red devils'?
   A. They spray a red ink.
   B. They can grow as large as six feet.
   C. They live at great depths in the ocean.
   D. They can be very aggressive.

2. Which word on page 7 is closest in meaning to 'adventurous'?
   A. ferocious
   B. intrepid
   C. experienced
   D. plentiful

3. Which of the following does the fisherman claim on page 8?
   A. Red devils are deadly.
   B. Red devils completely ate his friend.
   C. Red devils taste good.
   D. Red devils jump on boats.

4. Cranston may need _____ a couple of dives to see a squid.
   A. less than
   B. nonetheless
   C. at least
   D. undergo

5. A rebreather does all of the following EXCEPT:
   A. filters out carbon dioxide
   B. lets a diver stay down for 11 hours
   C. warns a diver when oxygen levels are low
   D. adds oxygen to a diver's inhaled breaths

6. Which of these questions CAN be answered with the information provided on page 15?
   A. At what time precisely do Humboldt squid begin to rise up from depths of 180 meters?
   B. What is the deepest depth that a human diver can go to?
   C. What color is generally not visible under the sea?
   D. What is Cranston wearing so the squid won't see him?

7. About which of the following does Cranston express worry on page 16?
   A. breathing in carbon dioxide
   B. being eaten by a squid
   C. getting sleepy during the long dive
   D. being without his diving equipment underwater

8. On page 18, 'a dangerous commitment,' refers to:
   A. using a rebreather
   B. researching giant squid
   C. going so deep underwater
   D. bringing a camera into the sea

9. Which of the following is NOT a suitable heading for page 21?
   A. Cameraman Vulnerable as Group of Squid Attack
   B. Giant Squid Cease Movement When Red Light Appears
   C. No casualties in Underwater Battle
   D. Man in Danger Due to Giant Squid

10. What does the writer claim about Cranston on page 22?
   A. He is modest.
   B. He is frank.
   C. He is coordinated.
   D. He is considerate.

11. Watching the encounter on the small screen is fascinating _____ the scientist.
   A. of
   B. with
   C. in
   D. for

12. Which of the following opinions does Dr. Bob Gilly express on page 26?
   A. He is jealous of Cranston's experience.
   B. He is thankful to Cranston for his film.
   C. He is amazed by the intelligent behavior of the squid.
   D. He is anxious to go diving to see the red devils.

The Jumbo vs. The Colossal Squid

Squid are among the least understood of all invertebrates. For centuries sailors have reported squid-like monsters so large that they would be capable of destroying entire ships. Only recently, however, have biologists been able to determine the truth about these strange creatures. They are also now able to categorize many of them by genus, a more general category of animal types, as well as by species. Two such enormous squid are the jumbo squid and the colossal squid.

The Jumbo Squid

The jumbo squid, also known as the Humboldt squid, has been sighted in the Pacific Ocean from the tip of South America to the coast of California. Recently, some have appeared as far north as Alaska, raising questions about the effects of global warming on the species. Some researchers suggest that they are moving further north because the northern oceans are warming, while others believe that declining numbers of predators have allowed the jumbo squid to expand their territories.

One unusual feature of the jumbo squid is its ability to radically change its color from reddish-purple to pure white. The red color is useful to the squid when hunting for food since red is not easily visible to fish and other creatures in the darkness of the ocean depths. This species is also known to be quite aggressive and Mexican divers who have encountered them underwater have given them the name *diablos rojos*, or 'red devils.'

The Colossal Squid

For many years, little was known about the species of squid called the 'colossal squid.' It was first identified in 1925 when scientists discovered two huge squid tentacles in a whale's stomach. The term 'colossal squid' was

Comparison of the Jumbo and Colossal Squid

Information	Jumbo Squid (Humboldt Squid)	Colossal Squid
Genus and Species	*Dosidicus gigas*	*Mesonychoteuthis hamiltoni*
Maximum Size	2 meters long	14 meters long
Maximum Weight	45 kilograms	unknown
Ocean Depth Range	200 to 700 meters	deeper than 2200 meters
Habitat	Eastern Pacific Ocean	Antarctic Ocean region
Special Features	can change color	movable hooks on tentacles

created in 2004 when a group of fishermen off the coast of New Zealand accidentally caught a six-meter-long squid. They took their find to a research center where experts confirmed that it was indeed an example of the largest species of squid known to science. The word 'colossal' was used to distinguish it from its smaller relative, the giant squid. Although scientists had examined similar squid in the past, those animals were found dead and their bodies were not complete or in good condition. The researchers in New Zealand were extremely excited because this was only the second time in history that scientists were provided with the opportunity to do a thorough examination of an undamaged example of a colossal squid.

CD 1, Track 04

Word Count: 392
Time: _____

Vocabulary List

camouflage (15)
carnivorous (2, 8)
decompression sickness (3, 18)
dusk (15)
dwell (15)
eerie (18)
ferocious (7, 16)
filter (3, 12, 25)
gauge (12)
grab a hold of (something) (22, 25)
hose (16, 18)
ink (2, 22, 25)
intrepid (3, 7)
invertebrate (2, 4, 8, 15)
jumbo (8, 15)
neurobiologist (3, 4)
predator (2, 3, 22)
prey (2, 3, 25)
scuba (3, 11, 18)
squirt (2, 22)
superb (26)
tag (4)
tentacle (2, 3, 8, 21, 22)

Metric Conversion Chart

Area
1 hectare = 2.471 acres

Length
1 centimeter = .394 inches
1 meter = 1.094 yards
1 kilometer = .621 miles

Temperature
0° Celsius = 32° Fahrenheit

Volume
1 liter = 1.057 quarts

Weight
1 gram = .035 ounces
1 kilogram = 2.2 pounds